Ghost and Shadow Towns of the Glory Road

This sightless window socket staring, watches
and broods. In disarray, bleary with neglect, it
eyes our intrusion.

GHOST
of the GLORY ROAD

south brunswick and new york: a. s. barnes and company

london: thomas yoseloff ltd

and SHADOW TOWNS

a photographic quest
by THOMAS MOORE

© 1970 by A. S. Barnes and Co., Inc.
Library of Congress Catalogue Card Number: 76-92040

A. S. Barnes and Co., Inc.
Cranbury, New Jersey 08512

Thomas Yoseloff Ltd
108 New Bond Street
London W1Y OQX, England

Mr. Moore is also the author of Bodie: Ghost Town

SBN: 498 07427 7
Printed in the United States of America

To
Nel Murbarger
who preceded me to all these places
and sang a compelling siren song of people
and places of an era I could never have imagined.
Now, even better than imagination, I have experienced
a little of the joy, exhilaration and
pathos that came to those who first walked the
Glory Road.

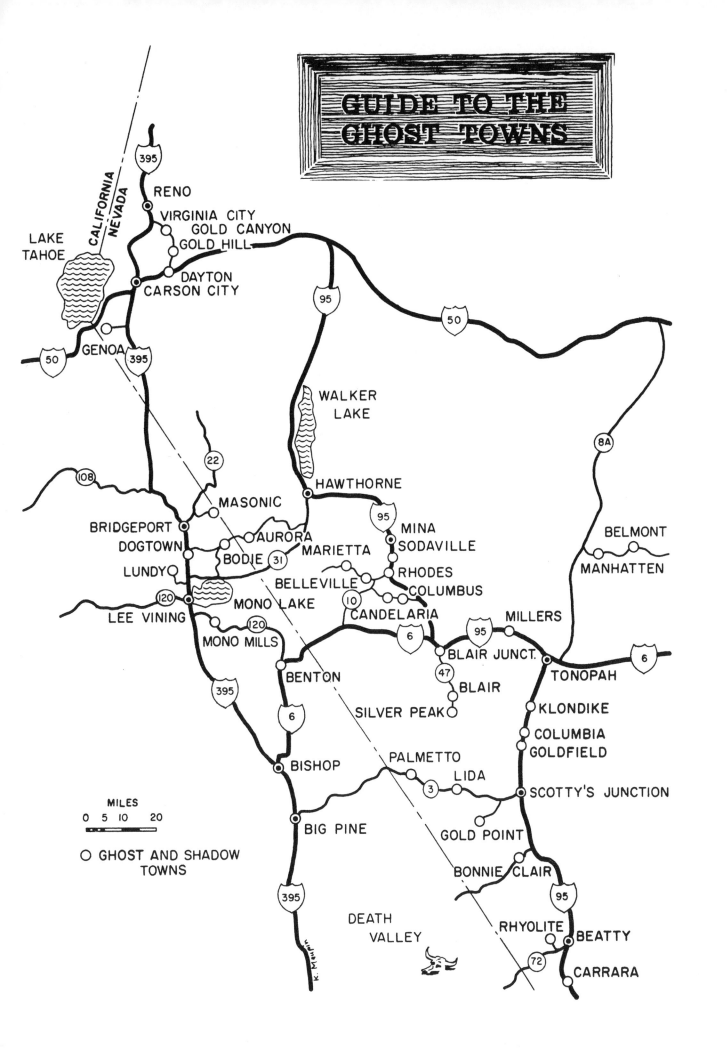

Ghost and Shadow Towns of the Glory Road

I beheld, and, lo, there was no man, and all the birds of the heavens were fled. I beheld, and lo, the fruitful place was a wilderness, and all the cities thereof were broken down at the presence of the Lord, and by His fierce anger. For thus hath the Lord said, "The whole land shall be desolate; yet will I not make a full end."

Jeremiah 4:25–27

Prologue

Aloneness and the Sourdough! It was not a despairing loneliness because he had his dream, he had his burro, and he talked—sometimes to himself, sometimes to his burro, and sometimes to the trees, the sky, and the birds. When he was out there in the mountains for long periods of time, the trees, the sky, the birds and the burro talked back in windsong, warbles and reassuring nods.

Mountain walls closed in on me as I cautiously drove the tortuous nineteen miles to the abandoned town. I began to feel the complete isolation and the utter dependency upon the vehicle beneath me. Gold! It drove a nation to frenzy when the cry was sounded. People streamed down this canyon trail and it became a road. Thief, tradesman, merchant and harlot all had a common bond. Once that cry was sounded, there were people. But before the news there was nothing around here for fifty miles—not even this road. Why would a man and his burro turn in here? In all of Nevada why this place? Alone, lacking all physical comforts, little water, little food, his wife and children praying for him back in Poughkeepsie or Baltimore, this man chose to abandon all to gain that precious metal.

When a miner found gold he talked! A little "showin" in the ore and a few drinks to celebrate his find when he did return to town and the crowd, merchant, harlot and speculator, would stampede to his diggin's. Thus a new town was born.

These towns all began the same way, flourished the same way and died the same way. Some are indeed quite dead. Some are ghostly and have only a sense of presence. Others, though occupied, are only shadows now of former greatness. These are pages of "then" and "now" contrasts. They tell you what the boom towns were then—and show you what the ghosts and shadows are now.

Lundy, Calfornia

Originally a lumber camp in 1878 supplying timber for Bodie 20 miles to the east, Lundy had a population peak of 3,000, and a Main Street four blocks long. Gold was discovered on the mountainside and the "May Lundy" mine was formed. There were other mines, but frequent mountain slides made them dangerous to work and eventually washed them all into beautiful Lundy Lake. There is now only good fishing at this shadow town.

Main Street: once it extended out over the waters of the lake by boardwalk. There were shops and saloons on both sides of it, but now it has shriveled to the water's edge.

14

The Monoville post office building has become a private home in Lundy.

A Lundy "original" awaits its fate at the hands of vandals and souvenir hunters, and the onslaughts of winter.

19

Bodie, California

Queen of ghost towns, Bodie was once a mining metropolis. Twenty thousand people lived here in 1878. They supported sixty saloons and gambling halls, three breweries and three local newspapers. "Shooters Town" produced over $100 million in high grade ore. Unknown by most, overland transmission of electrical power was first used here, but the euphemism, "I'm a Bad Man from Bodie" was known around the world.

False fronted "Bodie Moikes" saloon faces the morning sun as Main street stretches and rises to face another day—for what?

20

Resting tipsily on the line of demarcation between Bodie respectability and the red light district, the jail with its worn floor and little cell bunks was the busiest rooming house in town.

"Shooter's town," "the Bad Man from Bodie," "a dead man for breakfast," all are phrases attesting to Bodie toughness. 'Tis said, a hangin' or a church will kill any mining town. Bodie had both.

Aurora, Nevada

Named "Golden City of the Dawn" by those who first discovered her as a beautifully preserved ghost town, Aurora still had over 100 buildings of brick, and stone with wood filigree. Brick thieves reduced the memorial to these few shacks. Founded in 1860, Aurora knew violence in the beginning from the hanging of the Dailey gang to the present-day scavengers. Six thousand people lived here in 1864, including her most famous citizen, Mark Twain. Her large business district built of bricks and stone included a dozen hotels—one three stories!—and two dozen boarding houses, two newspapers, two armories, two dozen saloons and a red light district. Aurora was born at a time when there was not a single mile of railroad track in the state. Every brick, every powder round fired in the mines, every stamp for her eighteen large mills, every window and door was freighted over the lofty Sierra mountains from Sacramento by ox team. Aurora was unique. The City of the Dawn functioned for 2½ years as the seat of Esmeralda County in Nevada and the seat of Mono County in California—simultaneously—until the boundary was surveyed. Aurora's gold was shallow and her veins, though rich, petered out quickly. The town died in 1883 when she lost her courthouse to Hawthorne.

Rest in peace, Mrs. Mary Reid, it has been lo these many years. There is shade from the desert sun at last.

Of the deserted ghost towns included in this book, Aurora was the least friendly and most uninviting—yet no one was there!

29

Dogtown, California

The "eastern" gold rush started here. Prospectors who became discouraged with the diggin's in California began to spill back over the great Sierra Nevada mountains. The first major strike occurred in this area when young Cord Norst from Germany and his pretty Indian wife began panning placer gold in what he called Dogtown Creek. In 1857, Mormons in Nevada and later some from California moved into the area. It was always a small settlement with a general store and homes just dugouts—hovels against the hill—hence the name Dogtown. A man known only as Chris, attempting to sober up, walked into the hills near Dogtown. When he stumbled and fell, his hands clutched the dirt beneath him—gold! Monoville was born. They came eastward, then, from the California Mother Lode and founded the towns with their strikes. Bodie, Aurora, Candelaria, they founded all the gold towns in the Great Sink. These huts, humble and isolated as they are, mark the most peaceful of all the ghost towns.

Across the stream, tumbled against the foot of the hill, is all that is left of a town that was built before the Civil war.

DOG TOWN
1857

SITE OF THE FIRST MAJOR GOLD RUSH TO CALIFORNIAS
EASTERN SLOPE OF THE SIERRA NEVADA. DOG TOWN
DERIVED ITS NAME FROM A POPULAR MINERS TERM
FOR CAMPS WITH HUTS OR HOVELS. RUINS LYING
CLOSE TO THE CLIFF BORDERING DOG TOWN CREEK
ARE ALL THAT REMAIN OF THE MAKESHIFT DWELLINGS
WHICH HERE FORMED PART OF THE "DIGGINS"

CALIFORNIA REGISTERED HISTORICAL LANDMARK NO 792

PLAQUE PLACED BY THE CALIFORNIA STATE PARK
COMMISSION IN COOPERATION WITH THE MONO COUNTY
DEPARTMENT OF PARKS AND RECREATION AND THE
MONO COUNTY HISTORICAL SOCIETY SEPTEMBER II 1964

The home of Norst in the golden autumn morning light seems almost cheerful. The silence is a warm silence, but chill darkness comes quickly in the mountains.

Masonic, California

Really three towns in one, Masonic boasted three groceries, a post office and two hotels for her population of 600. This populace was supported by the "Pittsburgh," "Liberty" and "Jump-Up-Joe" mines. High overhead cables were used to carry ore from mine to mill and rattled continuously day and night. Although founded in the 1860s, Masonic had an active mining population through 1905. Today only ghosts live here.

Upper Town homes of the elite, now ghost homes leaning against the mountainside—doddering.

A Middle Town hotel? Sure, any building with more than two windows on a side was a hotel.

Lower Town and mill—a swinging place with cables and ore buckets constantly rattling and swaying overhead.

Benton, California

Formerly known as Benton Station, this was the southern terminus of the Carson, Bodie Stage and the anticipated junction for the Carson & Colorado and the Bodie & Benton Railroads. The town, though failing, was caught up in the web of Tonopah and Goldfield, as these twentieth-century boomtowns sought to tap the lumber resources of the Mono Mills area. But Benton started as a gold town in 1865 and served as the commercial center for the Montgomery, Mammoth and southern Mono mining districts. It was here that Black Taylor, partner of William Bodey (the discoverer of Bodie), was attacked in his cabin by a war party of Piute Indians. Taylor managed to kill ten braves before he was dragged from the cabin and, amid shouts and yells, his head was severed from his body. Benton still functions as a terminus of sorts as its shadows darken.

A desert oasis squatting in the shimmering heat, this crossroads town is no longer at the vital crossroads and it will die.

The Benton Hotel has many vacancies these days.

A residential street in Benton still conveys a feeling of ghostly neighborliness.

Wall detail showing board-and-batten house construction and the family stew pot.

Cuprite, Nevada

In 1908 this was the nearest railroad town to thriving gold towns of Lida, Gold Point, Bonnie Clare and Tule Canyon. This terminus was the extension of the railroad from Goldfield and Tonopah. Though it grew and prospered, it had no economy of its own. When the aforementioned towns began to fade, Cuprite did likewise albeit more quickly. Strewn rubble, bricks and bottles are all that attest to its existence.

Gone, all gone. Those towns that had the least root are the most completely leveled. A hundred cars drive by each day and none know of this bit of history, west.

"Bachelor button" washers were used to nail paper or balloon cloth to the inside rough wooden walls of these homes to keep out the chill desert winds. These at Cuprite are typical of every ghost town.

Blair, Nevada

Once the location of Nevada's largest—120 stamps—ore mill, this ghost town had a water and sewer system, a weekly newspaper, a two-story hotel, a bank and many stores in 1907. Blair was served by the Silver Peak Railroad, which connected with the Tonopah & Goldfield Railroad at Blair Junction.

Bones of cow and city bleach and bake under the merciless Nevada sun, both having died from the same reason—lack of sustenance.

Overlooking another salt marsh 47 miles from Columbus, Blair was a modern city—with indoor plumbing and sewers.

Blair Junction, where the Silver Peak railroad serving Blair connected with the Tonopah and Goldfield railroad. It was a typical railroad town and a sporting place for the elite town of Blair thirteen miles to the south.

Candelaria, Nevada

Founded by Mexicans and named for the day of Candle Mass, the town knew nothing of reverence or churches. This raw city, which began in 1863, was tough, parched, barren and lawless. Its foreign-born outnumbered American citizenry four to one. The silver mines of this region supported ten saloons, two hotels, doctors, lawyers and two newspapers—the *Chloride Belt* and the *True Fissure*. Candelaria was a most unhealthy place to live as one was forced to endure dust, flies and lack of water. Miners worked ten hours a day, seven days a week. The town died in a battle over wages and is truly a ghost town.

Ore, freight and borax wagons rumbled down this main street every hour of the day and red dust deep enough to cover the horses' hoofs lay over the town.

Mr. Gaunce died in the prime of life and town. The Northern Belle had produced almost $15 million in silver ore and Candelaria was the largest town in Esmeralda County.

The bank stands forlornly beside the main street as we look toward the Columbus borax marsh and its mine of pure castile soap. It is ironic that water at one time sold for one dollar a gallon midst all this fine soap.

Klondike, Nevada

This was a small gold town which had its beginning in 1899. Jim Butler was bound for this place when he made his historic strike that created Tonopah. Thereafter, located midway between Tonopah and Goldfield, Klondike was a station-stop on the railroad connecting the two boom towns. Along with a complete business section, Klondike supported a post office. Though never a large community, the town supplied the early needs of the new strike at Tonopah and died in the shadow of the eclipse.

The Klondike water hole presided over by curious cattle. It is hard to believe a thriving town once stood right here.

Tonopah, Nevada

A silver mining center during the boom years of 1908–1910 with 14,000 people, Tonopah also served as the hub of Nevada's twentieth-century mining industry by sending out rail and stage tentacles in all directions. South to Klondike, Goldfield and Cuprite; north to Manhattan, east to Clifford and west to Sodaville, Blair, Silver Peak, faded Bodie and lumber rich Mono Mills; these were a few of the stops along the glory road. Tonopah had its boom-town beginning in 1900 when Jim Butler discovered some promising outcroppings on nearby Sawtooth Peak. While this beginning was so typical, there was a sense of permanence. And, as the phoenix rose anew from the ashes of its past, so Tonopah thrusts new buildings through clusters of old 1908 miners' shacks and tailing dumps. Tonopah wears her birth scars proudly.

Slouching in the saddle between Mount Butler and Mount Oddie, formerly Sawtooth Peak, Tonopah has become a serious city from a frivolous boom camp.

Squatting in the afternoon sun like a drowsy mud turtle this mud adobe watches the source of the new prosperity—the radar installation at the mountaintop.

68

A short block from the main street, in the back yard of the business district, stand these 1905 houses filled to overflowing with furniture, trunks and newspapers of the era when Tonopah was the largest city.

Goldfield, Nevada

Though gold was discovered here at "Grandpa" by Harry Stimler and William Marsh in December of 1902, the rush did not occur until a year later when high grade ore began to show up. The name was changed to Goldfield and the boom was on. By 1908 the population had soared to 20,000. Through the years from 1903 to 1921 almost $85 million in high-grade ore was produced from this region. Goldfield was a freewheeling, high spirited town often requiring troops to quiet its turbulence and labor troubles. On Labor Day in 1906, Joe Gans, lightweight champion, defeated Battling Nelson for the largest purse yet offered for a prizefight. Goldfield is a shadow now of former greatness, but hope springs eternal. You can buy a downtown lot for $300.

This curious mountain identifies Goldfield from all directions because the peak shows the same contour regardless of the approach to the town. This is the edge of town looking north.

The school and courthouse show classic early-twentieth-century architecture. Behind the gaunt frame house is "The Hotel," an imposing 150-room, five story brick structure that housed a hundred families during World War II. It was finally closed in 1946 and never made a dime for its owners.

Belmont, Nevada

Such a promising city in the 1860s, Belmont was able to wrest the seat of Nye County government from Ione—building a stately courthouse to house it. A silver town with an extensive business district, Belmont accommodated 10,000 residents in 1867. Hot blood between the Cornish and Irish boomers helped provide Belmont's share of violence which also included the lynching of McIntyre and Walker by the "301" vigilantes. District Attorney Jim Butler inadvertently led to the town's demise in 1900. Leaving his office duties to his assistant, Tasker L. Oddie, later governor of the state, he traveled south toward Klondike. While camped at a place called Tonopah Springs, he made one of the greatest strikes in Nevada history which drained Belmont's sagging population over night. Today Belmont is only a shadow town with her summer population of four, her dream of power and her stately remnant of grandeur.

Teetering precariously in the summer sun this remnant will be toppled before the year end. Thus the buildings crumble. Thus the towns die.

Cultural center of Belmont was the Cosmopolitan Hall. Such famous theatrical names as the Chapman Family, Amy Stone and child star Fay Templeton were billed through the late 1860s and early 1870s. Now sun streaming through a hole in the roof and reflecting from a wall creates an illusion of light and life in the building.

Belmont is proud still of her stately courthouse.
Every brick, lime, mortar, concrete and stone
had been fired and quarried from surrounding
canyons.

Carrara, Nevada

Just a step from the glory trail but a ghost town nevertheless, Carrara, named for Michelangelo's marble city in Italy, sustained life from 1904 to 1936. Fine marble was quarried here in the beginning. The quality finally degenerated, eventually became too fractured for use and the town died.

A young ghost town as ghost towns are chronicled, but as stark, as silent and as foreboding as the oldest. Carrara clutches the mountainside with brick and mortar permanence that tells me it will be here even after I'm gone.

Looking across the somber Amargosa desert and Death Valley beyond that, these ruins are a grey shelter for repulsive grey lizards who scurry before you over grey gravel—they are the only inhabitants.

Manhattan, Nevada

Eclipsed by the big strikes at Tonopah and Goldfield in 1905, Manhattan nevertheless has a tale to tell. John Humphrey on a trip through the region broke off a few samples of rock by hand which brought him $3,000. The severe winters at nearly 7000 feet elevation did not slow the boom. The seven-block-long main street was solidly lined with business houses on both sides. Speculation in claims and city lots was very heavy. Property covered with snow was often never seen by its transitory owner. Shortly after the slaying of Sheriff Tom Logan by Walter Barieu, the city received a shock from an earthquake 300 miles away. The speculative mines had been backed by San Francisco capital, which was suddenly withdrawn. Manhattan survived and by 1912 the town was booming again—for a little while. In 1938 the world's second largest electric powered bucket dredge was commissioned to gobble the gravel of Manhattan Gulch. It ceased operation in 1946 leaving behind mountains of tailing waste. The town is not a ghost town and resents any implication as such—but the shadows are lengthening.

The Manhattan Literary Society building erected by fourteen members, one of whom is still alive. The building is still on the tax rolls.

The Manhattan Fire Department on the main street. It was not too efficient as there were seven, 5- to 7-story buildings in the town— but not today.

Standing somber and dark in the Mount Moriah Cemetery, the headboard of Mrs. McFadden tells us she died between the boom years of this town that refused to die. There was a beginning in 1866, a boom in 1905 and 1912, a revival in 1915 and again in 1938.

Goldpoint, Nevada

Founded in the early 1900s as Hornsilver, there were high hopes for this new camp. *The Goldfield Review* on May 30, 1908, said, "Hornsilver is the latest wonder in Nevada mining districts . . . Main Street is extending as you watch it . . ." Hornsilver had thirteen saloons, supported *The Herald,* a weekly newspaper, eight restaurants, several hotels and an auto transportation company furnishing access to Goldfield at $7.50 and Cuprite at $5.00 per trip. Hornsilver changed her name in 1920 to attract investment, but could not stem the erosion that saw the population shrivel from 2000 people to a shadowy six. Goldpoint serves as a threshold to ghost towns of Gold Mountain and Oriental, nine miles to the south and west.

Dusty and dry in the late morning sun, isolated from any prospering village or town, it was disconcerting to hear organ music introducing a popular T.V. soap opera with its well-modulated character voices.

Backs to the sun, standing darkly, these buildings anchor the western side of a main street
that seems to run in a circle. All the buildings
in the town are unusually black and so show
darkly against the sun bleached ground.

The eastern side of the circle shows window-less houses that must have been insufferably hot in summer and shivering cold in winter. In all of these towns firewood was precious, but never more so than gold.

Silver Peak, Nevada

Located in the center of Esmeralda mining districts since 1864, Silver Peak was once one of the leading mining towns in the state. The town was a stop on the Cluggage Stage Line serving Belmont, San Antone, Columbus, Lida and Gold Point. Later the camp was the terminus for the Silver Peak Railroad serving Tonopah and Goldfield. Silver Peak was a prosperous town with a good business district, a newspaper, *The Post,* and natural hot water. The town burned in 1948 but still supports both gold and silver mining. The old buildings declare a glorious past but the frenzied activity dispells any shadows that would lengthen.

The Post Office: the walls are lined with posters of wanted desperadoes; the floor and steps are worn thin by countless miners' boots. This original building still serves as a far-flung outpost of the Federal System.

Fashioned from shingles, tar paper, adobe and bottles, this home in downtown Silver Peak has only recently been abandoned. The lump of Silver Peak rises nakedly in the background.

His and Hers—this bathhouse, with both tubs intact, stands starkly on the borax-covered, cesspool-laced valley floor. The intimidation must have been considerable with twenty grimey miners lined up by the men's entrance and perhaps two or three ladies awaiting at the other door.

While standing in the women's bathtub, milady could look toward the great cities to the East, but she would see only the borax marsh of Silver Peak, hear the rough talk of the miners in the adjoining room and wonder about her existence in this difficult place.

Mono Mills, California

Though founded as early as 1872, lumber town Mono Mills did not really boom until the Bodie Railway and Lumber Company was organized in 1881. This settlement became the center of a large lumbering and cordwood operation that served many of the mining camps of southern Nevada, including later towns of Tonopah, Sodaville and Goldfield. The population had a large percentage of Chinese and Piute Indians who worked for the railroad and mills in the summer but drifted to various places in the Mono Basin during the fall and winter months.

There were shootings and stabbings here too, but that sense of presence seems different somehow in this beautifully wooded area. Are miners' ghosts different than lumbermen's ghosts?

A photographic study of texture and composition in a saw mill hoist pulley long ago stripped of its iron to feed the demands of a nation in its first World War. The rails and four railroad engines were likewise consumed.

108

Marietta, Nevada

Marietta was founded in 1867 when salt harvesting began in Teel's Marsh. The town knew its boom days in 1873 when borax mining and a plant for processing it came into being. When salt was the main product, it was shipped to the silver mills of the great Comstock area by camel train and also to Aurora by pack mules.

The road coming in from the right leads to the town squatting in the salt and borax marsh. The road continues over the mountains west to Aurora.

The Marietta Post Office stands weary and sightless, accepting the relentless onslaughts of winter wind and summer sun—and time.

This was Marietta's biggest hardware store, or rather, general store in those days. Completely surrounded by bleak, overpowering mountains, a merchant often erected such an edifice to measure himself against those very mountains.

Rhodes, Nevada

This is one of seven sin and silver centers founded in the years 1863–1873 on the borax flats between the Excelsior and Monte Cristo Ranges. Rhodes was originally a borax town. Later it became a station on the Carson and Colorado Railroad.

Fashioned of natural flat sided stone, this house required many years to build. The chromatic range of the many colored rocks was heightened by the polishing action of wind and dust, and the brilliance of the desert sun.

Sodaville, Nevada

Once the most important town between Tonopah and Reno, Sodaville was a thriving rail terminus in 1904, as well as a mining town in its own right beginning in 1873. It was the connecting point for the Tonopah Railroad and the Carson and Colorado Railroad. The town had a peak population of 3000 and was the largest settlement in Mineral County. The first tungsten mine in the United States was located here. Started by the Germans, the mine and mill were abandoned in 1914 at the start of World War I.

Virtually nothing left but two old homes, one loaded with a widow's fine furniture of another era, the other fixed up and treasured by a couple from New Jersey, who love this barren land.

Sodaville Mill: once crushing ore from Candelaria, Belleville, Columbus, Marietta and Pickhandle Gulch, it now stands guard over this portion of the Nevada desert like some far-flung Legion outpost, somber and crumbling.

121

Belleville, Nevada

Spawned into being by the Northern Belle's new mill in 1873, Belleville was a milling and shipping center for the six mining towns surrounding it. Primarily a mill town with a second 20 stamp mill added in 1876, Belleville's central location greatly aided its reputation as one of the best "sporting towns" in Nevada. There were many hotels, seven saloons and two newspapers. Belleville was the scene of a regular main street fast-draw shootout when Ramon Montenegro, owner of the Club House, the leading palace of pleasure, squared off with Judge A. G. Turner. When the staccato barks of gunfire subsided, Montenegro sank to his knees with two slugs in his belly, looked at his genteel foe in disbelief, then pitched forward headlong into the dust of history as did Belleville in 1882.

Belleville's traces are almost buried by this sudden sea of mud washed in by a cloudburst in 1966. Could this have been the only cloudburst since 1873?

Bonnie Clare, Nevada

Smallest of the mining towns of the early twentieth century, Bonnie Clare was in direct competition with the towns of Lida, Hornsilver and Tule Canyon in 1908–1909. The camp's proximity to Cuprite, the rail center servicing these new towns, probably cleaned out its gold the quickest.

It was eerie—who could be here and whistling? I shouted a shaken halloo! The whistling and my answering halloo continued as I approached the town. Suddenly I felt very foolish—and relieved. Standing near the corner of the barracks I could both see and hear the cause of the whistle. The edge of the metal roof curled back upon itself and screeched that eerie whistle each time the wind gusted. I was physically alone indeed.

Columbus, Nevada

A sister town to Candelaria, Columbus started as a salt mining town in 1865. This commodity was required for the chlorination milling of Candelaria's silver. William Troop, a former Comstock miner, discovered that the silky white stuff covering the marsh was pure borax and by 1872, the town was prospering from the production and refining of cottonball borax. Francis Marion "Borax" Smith established the Pacific Coast Borax Company, originated the famous "Twenty-Mule Team" trademark and built the Tonopah and Tidewater Railroad. The town knew its greatest prosperity from 1870 to 1875 when it boasted two newspapers, an iron foundry, machine shops, Holland's Hotel, 1000 Chinese, and the lynching of Victor Monega.

The last cabin left in the hills above Columbus, that of a gold and silver miner, attests to the variety of mineral deposits in this desert country. In all this vastness, one needs only to decide where to start digging.

Genoa, Nevada

Originally called Reeses Station and later Mormon Station, this is the oldest town in Nevada, at that time Utah Territory, founded in 1849. Hampden S. Beattie built the first house in the territory. The name was changed to Genoa after the birth place of Christopher Columbus. *The Territorial Enterprise,* newspaper of Mark Twain fame, had its beginning here in 1858 and was later moved to Virginia City in 1860. As Mormon Station, this town was the beginning of Mormon colonization of the Carson Valley and the founding of the Utah Territorial government.

Genoa Bar, Nevada's oldest known thirst parlor, is still satisfying thirst. Predecessor of a hundred thousand such establishments in the state, Genoa Bar was a regal saloon in its heyday.

This was formerly the Douglas County courthouse, rebuilt on the site of the first courthouse built in Nevada, which had burned in 1911. The building functions today as the district elementary school.

131

Amid the surrounding mementos of a bygone era, Annabell and Leo Andres dispense drinks in the same hearty manner of barkeeps before them. In the old days the "free lunch," an institution which began in San Francisco, reached its zenith on the Comstock. Casualness and restraint were the prerequisites to a successful foray on the stack of sandwiches, eggs and pretzels sitting on the bar.

Lida, Nevada

Founded in 1872, the town barely struggled along for thirty years. Over 187 miles from the nearest railroad at Cuprite, the isolation of Lida almost choked it until a gold ledge was discovered in 1904. *The Lida Enterprise* was published and a water pipe line was surveyed from neighboring Gold Point. The town character, "Old Len Martin," now unwashed and unshaven, drunk and degenerate, in his younger days once faced three armed robbers while on a trip to Palmetto. Though unarmed at the time, he broke a branch from a juniper tree and soundly clubbed his assailants. Like Old Len, Lida's glory was brief. The town sits in a tree shaded valley, stricken in years and vigor.

Main Street once extended past this home and that tree was just a newly planted sapling when the boom was on in Lida. We are looking West toward Palmetto and California beyond.

Lida was already starting to fade when Rebecca died in 1907. But Lida is not dead—a shadow of her former self perhaps, but not dead. The spirited thoroughbred horses being raised in this region do not allow one to think of ghosts.

Franktown, Nevada

This is the second town settled in Nevada. It was an important milling town for the Comstock ores and was named for Francois Poirier. The town is one of a string of little pearls from Reno south to Carson City, as are Steamboat Springs, Washoe City and Ophir City. Close by is the mansion of Sandy Bowers.

Situated in a park-like grove of trees, this country school has not been so long abandoned. It served the Franktown district educational needs, often with grades one to twelve being taught in the same room by the same teacher. (*See illustration on page 140*)

Sandy and Eilly Bowers, poor when they married, built this fabulous home after selling off their mining stock, which they had received as wages. Though considered valueless at the time they received it, fantastically rich ore was discovered which zoomed their holdings to over a million dollars. Crafty Sandy and Eilly sold out and became the first actual millionaires of the Comstock. Sandy died at age 35 and the fortune dwindled to nothing. In later years, Eilly eked out a precarious existance as a seeress and fortune teller. She who had been presented to Queen Victoria of England died in poverty. Solid silver door knobs, hinges and opulent furnishings long before had been stripped from the building. (*See illustration on page 141*)

Palmetto, Nevada

Born in 1866, Palmetto had leases on life renewed in 1880 and again in 1900. The town's Main Street was a mile long in 1906. There were offices, hotels, saloons, a Post Office, bank, newspaper (*The Herald*), and three stamp mills. Palmetto is on the Old Piper Toll Road built in the 1870s by Sam Piper of Fish Lake Valley, linking the bustling mining centers of Tule Canyon, Lida and Gold Mountain.

The Palmetto district is arid, open and treeless, pocked with mounds of tailings like a dried up lawn spotted with gopher mounds.

An ore loading dock stands starkly against the cloudless sky. Silent, crumbling, awaiting erasure by time—is there no more gold here?

Ruins of the Palmetto mill office show a fine example of adobe construction. The only native building material available besides stone, these buildings were cool in summer, warm in winter, and dark in summer and winter.

Millers, Nevada

Millers functioned mostly as a milling town for Tonapah ore and its prosperity coincided with that of its 13-mile neighbor. Gold was discovered here however, and as soon as the word was spread, one could see fancy dressed dandies and girls from dance halls in Tonapah—high heels and all—digging for that golden metal. The town had a Post Office, as well as a substantial business district in 1907.

This tattered cabin, its insides flapping in the hot wind like a washday shirt, tells of the harsh climate these people endured. Balloon cloth stretched across rough sawed lumber, filled with paste sizing, dried and papered, covered the inside chinks and knotholes. This kept the desert winds from snuffing out candles and lanterns. Suitable building materials were almost as valuable as the gold!

Millers was not too well laid out, being first
a milling center in 1907 and then a gold town.
The homes were never more than shelters lined
with balloon cloth. A dust devil kicks up a fuss,
dancing against the backdrop of the Gilbert
Mountain Range.

Rhyolite, Nevada

Once queen of all gold towns, Rhyolite had its beginning on a sizzling summer day in 1904 when young Eddie Cross from Iowa picked up a frog-shaped, greenish piece of ore. A few months later, the Bullfrog Mine was listed on the San Francisco exchange at $200,000! The boomers came from Tonopah, Goldfield, McWilliamstown (Las Vegas) and from the settlements along the Colorado. Looking down upon the hodgepodge that was now Bullfrog in 1905, Pete Busch dreamed and planned a lofty city on the mountainside. In less than a year, Golden Street, Rhyolite's main thoroughfare, was a wide, smooth, bustling artery with substantial two- and three-story buildings on both sides of it. This most arid location lying on the northern edge of the Amargosa Desert had three water companies serving it with good water pressure at all the city fire hydrants. By 1907, some of the ten hotels had menus offering oyster cocktails. Ten thousand people supported the 45 saloons, four newspapers, ice plant and opera house with wages ranging from $4.50 a day for mine labor to $10.00 a day for skills. But mostly Rhyolite was a speculation town and thus not able to weather the Panic of 1907. By 1911, the town truly died when the Montgomery-Shoshone mine failed.

This most elaborate depot in Nevada once served three railroads connecting to the Southern Pacific and the Atchison, Topeka and Santa Fe. After the boom, it became a casino and now functions as a rock shop and desert oasis for tourists, rock and bottle hounds.

The Porter brothers, who came to Rhyolite when the "buildings" were tents and the "streets" were rows of stakes, established this general store. By 1907, they owned real and personal property in excess of $150,000 in value, which grossed that same amount each month!

154

The First National Bank of Rhyolite, built during the height of the town's opulence, cost over $90,000. It seems incredible that the elements of wind, sun and rain could wreak such havoc on a concrete building in as little as sixty years. Steel was stripped from these hulks for two World Wars, but I wonder if their contribution was that significant.

The bank building housed numerous offices, including the Rhyolite Post Office. It seems that the towns that blossomed the quickest, decayed the quickest also. If the citizens of the great Silver State do not act quickly, these boom town monuments to a rich and strong pioneer heritage will soon be tumbled into the sage. Many towns already are just a small mound of broken bottles.

Rhyolite was justly proud of this fine school which sits and broods—windows staring across the Amargosa Desert and Death Valley beyond. As it was in other schools throughout the nation, students learned of geography and history, of other people and places. Do these other people and places learn of Rhyolite? I hope so.

Miners' homes were built of the most readily available materials. The Bottle House of Rhyolite was built of 51,000 whiskey bottles, a tribute to a monumental thirst. When assembled in the walls of this house, the bottles were clear and colorless. The sun has fired this desert kiln daily these many years to bake the glass a black purple hue.

163

Dayton, Nevada

Gold Canyon and the Comstock Lode began here at the intersection of Gold Canyon Creek and the Carson River. Originally Spafford Hall's Station, on the old 49er trail west, it was sometimes called Ponder's Rest as each California bound wagon train stopped to prepare itself for the assault on the Great Sierra Wall. The town was derisively called Chinatown after the Orientals who, imported by the Mormons to dig irrigation ditches at Genoa, deserted the farms to dig for gold and had banded together here for mutual protection. The West was difficult on anything that was different and many a Celestial was seen swinging from a tree branch strung up by his cue of hair. Gold was discovered here by William Prouse in 1850 and one placer miner washed out 600 ounces in one day, netting $8000! Strange blue stuff choked the rockers so most miners pushed on to the California Bonanza. Spafford Hall's Station became a stop for the Pony Express in 1860. That first pony brought news that the name of the Territory had been changed from Utah to Nevada with its seat of government placed in the Carson Valley.

Dayton Post Office, a significant improvement over Pony Express days, was built in 1891 and still functions. The Dayton Public School was built in 1865 and likewise functions to serve its original purpose.

165

Spafford Hall's Station was laid out by John Day, and for this feat the town was renamed Dayton in 1891. Nearby is the mouth of Sutro Tunnel, an engineering marvel in its day and monument to Adolph Sutro's persistence. It was used to drain steaming hot water from the Savage Mine. Now only memories are reason for the town's existence.

Silver City, Nevada

North from Dayton, up through Gold Canyon, past old Johntown, up to Silver City, the gold seekers came. It took nine years from the first discovery of gold at the mouth of the canyon to people it with 6000 souls. By 1864, the seven miles of Gold Canyon from Dayton to Virginia City formed one continuous metropolis. This is a part of the Comstock but unique because its mines produced mostly gold. The hated "blue stuff" of the Comstock region was found to be silver ore. It was natural then in this contrary land that Silver City would be famous for the first use of the cyanide process in 1894 for the production of gold at Donovan's Mill.

An endless stream of traffic passed up and down this road at all hours. Often at night a train of camels would be seen bringing in salt from Teal's Marsh to the mills on Sun Mountain. The trip was usually made at night because the camels frightened all the mules—the "Washoe Canaries."

169

Fire! With the scarcity of water in this harsh, dry land, this cry struck terror in the hearts of all who existed in the Canyon. The alarm was given by pulling the ring in the box that was tied to the bell clapper on the top of the fire house.

170

171

Gold Hill, Nevada

In the winter of 1858–59, "Old Virginny" Fennimore, who had been placer mining in Gold Canyon, saw a partially snow-covered red mound of gopher diggin's. The red outcropping was the clue. He plunged his hand deep into the gopher hole and pulled out a fist full of gold-flecked blue dirt. Gold Hill was born! The town prospered from the start. The day before the strike, Nick Ambrose had moved his bar up from Johntown, and Eilley Orrum and her boarders, including Sandy Bowers, helped move her boarding house next to the bar. By 1860, the first Miner's Union Hall in Nevada had been erected. There was the Bank of California, as well as schools, churches, lodge buildings and many substantial homes and offices. The town had a race track, and after 1870 there were trains every two hours to Virginia City and Carson City. The most famous mines were the Yellow Jacket, Crown Point and Belcher. Temperatures in these mines rose to over 100 degrees. In 1880 the New Yellow Jacket recorded a temperature of 170 degres at 3000 feet! In keeping with the contrary nature of the land and after the secret of the clogging "blue stuff" had been unlocked, Gold Hill became world famous as a producer of silver, second only to Virginia City.

The Virginia and Truckee railroad depot, Gold Hill. The tracks, which were sold for scrap in 1940, swept around the station across the snow patch to the right. Though no longer in existence here, the city's railroad trestle is given some degree of permanence, as it is enshrined on the great seal of the State of Nevada.

The Gold Hill Hotel, built in 1859, was the first hotel building on the Comstock. Earlier "hotels" were but tents, caves and dugouts. The walls are beginning to sag in spite of recent repairs and one observes anew that time ravages everything. How many thousands of people walked and rode past this edifice, up, ever upward toward the Queen of the Comstock?

174

All that remains of the Maynard Block. This was the heart of Gold Hill and included the Post Office, the Stock Exchange, dry goods, meat and grocery markets, French hair dresser, barber shop and doctors' offices. *The Gold Hill News* became as widely read as the *Territorial Enterprise* in Virginia City. Here in November's gloom the glory of a vigorous city becomes what it is—a pile of stones.

Looking across the Comstock for over 110 years, this window would support the observation made of Gold Hill in its early days that it is inconceivable that this region should ever have been designated as an abode for man. By 1880 Gold Hill was on the downgrade and on a doleful day in that year, Charlie Price's Bar posted this sign—"At Midnight, all drinks in this saloon are reduced to ten cents." Until then Gold Hill had boasted at least one two-bit saloon. With great and solemn ceremony, Alf Doten of *The Gold Hill News* bought the last two-bit drink as the town died peacefully.

179

Virginia City, Nevada

As the flood of gold seekers rose higher and higher in Gold Canyon, and after the winter's find at Gold Hill, Henry Comstock, braggart and loud-mouth, set about locating claims all over the area—"for ranching purposes," the notice said. In June, Pete O'Riley and Pat McLaughlin, with their day's pile of gold dust before them, were confronted by "Old Pancake" Comstock who accused them of trespassing. Intimidated, they settled for shares and the Ophir Company was formed. The town was duly christened on an October night in 1859 when "Old Virginny" Fennimore, wanted in California for murder, stumbled in the night and broke his bottle. Rising to his feet with drunken dignity, he poured the few remaining drops upon the sage and loudly proclaimed, "I baptize this spot Virginia Town." The baptism took and the wretched collection of huts and hovels became the Queen City of the Comstock Lode. In three years the city had a population of 15,000. The "damned blue stuff" was found to be rich silver ore and the cry "Silver in the Washoe" brought an endless stream of fortune seekers. By 1880, there were 20,000 people, some famous like Mark Twain, James Fair, John Mackay—who founded Mackay Radio—and George Hearst. There were the infamous, too, like Sam Brown who knifed sixteen men one winter; Judge David Terry, killer and rebel; and Julia Bulette, fairest rose of vice, murdered one night by Jean Milleain.

Nestled on the side of Sun Mountain, renamed Mount Davidson, the town lies shrunken now. St. Mary's of the Mountains thrusts a steepled hand heavenward. Built in 1860, the church had a bell of native silver in its belfry and an altar of marble from Carrara, Nevada.

From the Savage Mine Office south to the large Fourth Ward School stretches half the city. Everything was big in this town and it required two red light districts to satisfy the sporting element. There was the "Line" downtown on D Street and the Barbary Coast on C Street where the school building now stands. Like all mining towns, Virginia City had its disastrous fires, one in 1875 and another in 1883. Over the Divide, C Street continues south to Gold Hill, Silver City, Johntown, Dayton and Empire, a glory road of its own along the glory road of many.

In the fading light of a winter's day stands the Mackay Mansion, a memorial to the American Story. While the old guard of early discoverers died their tragic deaths—O'Riley in a madhouse, Old Virginny in the poor house and Comstock a suicide—a new breed rose to prominence on the Comstock. John Mackay started humbly in the lower canyon diggin's and took his wages in mining shares. After two decades, he was unable to estimate within 20 millions his real wealth. The partnership of Mackay, James Fair, James Flood and William O'Brien controlled the Comstock and brought to fruition the Great Silver Bonanza. John Mackay never forgot his humble beginning and gave much to the town, the poor and the unstaked.

184

Virginia City refused to be a ghost town though there are enough dead to make it so. In summer the old saloons still serve up the "tarantula juice" for the tourists, and the one-armed bandits noisily whirl their fruited dials as a curious nation throngs C Street. But in fall and winter the shadows lie darkly upon the land—lengthening. One last fire or a belching avalanche from Sun Mountain, and the town will be dead like all of the others.

Epilogue

The quest for gold was a hard life. Moving among these old ruins, ghosts and shadows, I am humbled by the circumstances of hardship and deprivation these people endured. They were not the physical giants of western stories. They were little people. Coffins in the Bodie museum looked as if they had been made for children. Rooms and hallways in the better preserved homes were low, narrow and confining to me as I walked through them. A hotel lobby was no larger than the average single car garage—and about as gloomy. A log cabin home or tar paper shack for a family of four was half the size of that garage, but the life was a full one. Their energy was boundless and ennui was unknown. It took this drive to wrest a living from this barren land. When individual placer and pick mining effort gave way to hardrock and the corporation effort, the individualist packed his burro and searched anew. Those who stayed behind and mined for company wages built the towns with their needs, wants and desires. By actually experiencing these boom towns, one learns to understand and appreciate these people. The land *is* dry and a thirst builds quickly. If, in the assuagement of that thirst, one can build a rosy dream—or for a few moments suddenly feel big enough to match the vastness of a region that daily humbles him—why fault him? Miners have just never been able to work on soda pop. Small wonder then they were such hell raisers. The sense of isolation, alone in the mountains, or at the bottom of a cold dark mine shaft, was unnerving. He had to have the assurance of other beings in the world—by actual physical contact. If he didn't have the price of one of "those" girls in the houses on Maiden Lane, the next best thing was to get into a fight. Physical contact, laughter and the sound of his own voice became his touchstones with reality—the stronger and louder the better.

189

INDEX